Monstrous Cartography

poems

Robin Gow

new words {press}

A TRANS· & GENDER-EXPANSIVE POETRY PRESS

new words {press}
6030 Putnam Ave., New York, NY 11385
www.newwordspress.com | @newwordspress

new words {press} is a sponsored project of Fractured Atlas, a non-profit arts service organization with a mission of elevating emerging and established trans* and gender-expansive poetic voices, to build community, and share
knowledge.

ISBN: 979-8-9903488-3-7

Cover Art by Rain Black (fae/he)
Cover Design by brooklyn baggett
Typesetting by new words {press}

Printed in the United States of America

Table of Contents

The Cartographer's Lover

I have run out of answers to the question "how do we escape?"
You wake me up to alert me. We have stumbled
into the sea of teeth. I begged you again that we might get married
and live inside a cave. I bought you the eyes of every mermaid
I could find. There you were with your astrolabe. You said,
"I can see the life we crave." I said, "I can see how we die fabulously
and under the feet of a creature eight times the size of this boat."

Back Door Life

I keep it a secret where I sell my teeth.
Once, in the glow of a rotten flame
I saw a word for myself. It had
ten-thousand legs and it just
kept running. This is where
I welcome you. Where you come
to suck out my soul again just
so we can laugh and put it back.
Souls are not that serious. I had
a pet goldfish who talked directly
to god and I blew it. I could have
asked for anything but I just asked,
"Is there a clothing section for me?"
Liberation is when the house falls out
the back door. When there is a garden
you are not supposed to know about
bursting with round zucchini.
Bees with a queen living in their sound.
The butterfly bush has a pocket knife
and shakes me down for a quarter.
Gumballs for everyone daring. Key lime pie
for a furious hinge. It's always been
exhale exhale exhale. You do not
even have to knock.

A Thousand Tiny Sexes

I lived in a myth of realness. Touching and touching.
Carving my skin for a plastic baby. It is king's day.
It is a paper ship. It is a flaming mast. All the sailors
trying to be women in the dark. My sex like a grain
of rice in a wild bowl. How my hunger has eaten itself.
Full of sightlines. You can cut a porthole in anything
or anyone. I wanted one so badly. I wanted to walk
around and say, "I am a man" and have that be true.
Then I worshipped. Then everything was miniature
even my gender. The distance between gender and sex
becoming a false lake. Trick of the light and heat.
Running towards it and then legs gone. Then face gone.
Then only gender. Then the sex you keep in your pocket
for when the world is on fire and the other one you keep
as if it were ever true. I'm telling you it's small but it's still
as big as my life. I could crush it like a diet coke can.

Formerly Known As Identities

I'm not talking about the frilly socks
or even the way my body moves.

I am sick of writing and rewriting maps
to a place that does not exist.

Once, maybe, in the brevity of before-life
I was a gender but now I am just

exactly as I am. Sometimes when I am
inside my father's mouth again

and he is telling me I like it
I will be a boy. Sometimes when I am

eating with a plastic spoon
I will be debris. Refuse. Something discarded.

Until then and before then I have
no answers for you. What are my pronouns?

They are the dirt. They are what my breath
is made of. I have no language I want to use

as a push-pin. I have my tongue
and it is made of glass.

Globster

/
Let my body be
undefinable
when you come upon me
along the wanton surf.
I will tell you
what I am
if you promise
to not ask
any questions.

/
As a girl
I once drown
in the bathtub.
It took years
for my father to notice
that the body there
was mine or else
that is what he tells me
as he lifts me
and makes a puppet
of me.

/
Becoming so was the biggest relief.
No more eyes. No more mouth.
No more limbs to speak for. Just
a suggestion of what once was.
The waves crashing. Knuckles and nets.
Goodbye form. Goodbye classification
and species.

/
Tissue from a sperm whale. Tissue
passed from a father to a daughter
to a daughter to a son to whatever
the fuck I am. Tissue is such a soft word
for that which breaks. For that which
is entered and turned into flesh.

/
You promised me
you wouldn't
ask any questions.
You promised
you would
just listen.

/
Now you want to know where
and how I swallowed the anchor.
Now you want to know where
and how I ate men's legs.
Now you want to know where
and how he was able to do that to me.

/
Sometimes the answer
is an absence of words.
A perforation. Sometimes a drain.
Sometimes an answer
is just what's left of your body.
What are you? they ask.
Once, I knew.

Sea Pig

Eyes sprouted across my stomach. They were the four winds or they were my grandmother or they were you saying, "If only you were a boy." Then I was a boy and then I was a girl and then I was a sea pig standing in the surf. The sailors pointed and screamed as I tried to explain that all I wanted was a handful of figs. Once, I was looking in a mirror and the mirror became the ocean. Roaring glorious void. I fell in and never came out. I am still not out. A sea pig is not so much a gender but a place you go and do not leave. I tried to cut out the eyes. First with a spoon and then with a knife and then frantic with my fingers. They blinked. I thought I heard them moan. They are still there now. They hearing everything.

Anti-Coming Out Poem

When trying to name myself
I would cut off my fins each night
and sell them on the black market
to a group of men who believe
in subsisting on a diet of only other people's terror.

I bought a dictionary. I ate it
one page at a time. Maybe I am one
of those men. I bought socks with trans flags.
I tried to be a lesbian. I tried to be a twink.
I tried to be a bisexual. Then, I wondered
if I could be all and none of these cathedrals?

What if instead of being I was un-being.
Some kinds of rock form in layers. Sedimentary.
Shoulder after shoulder. I am clawing
the ground from my feet. I am walking
on water. I am no one vocabulary but my own
but then I am craving the little mini van.
The word "trans" has gills. Amphibial.
The fins always grow back. You are never
and always the beautiful monster.

Ziphius

Once, I drowned a bird
in the backyard
and it turned
into a whale. Once I stole
from my mother's wallet
and from the wallet
birds flew and flew
until I confessed.
I ate only powdered milk
until I felt pure again.
So much about being
is about un-being.
I try to say,
"this is not my body"
when I put on
my favorite dress.
Am I on my way
to becoming a nudist? Am I
on my way to drowning
another bird?
A bird is a symbol of freedom
only not in this poem.
In this poem a bird is
a symbol
for the part of the face
that doesn't belong
in the ocean. I had a priest
once call me "water owl."
He had boney cold hands.
Sometimes people ask me
"Are you alright?"
when they see I am not alright.
They are asking me to lie.
I will not lie, reader,
especially not to you.
I am the depths. I am what
cannot breathe. I eat men
and knit their bones
into stirrups.

Ode to Uncertainty

I do not know when I will die. I do not know
what to call my hands when I wake up. I do not know
how the birds manage to laugh in a time like this.
I do not know what name I would want
if I could name myself. You might say,
"You're trans, I thought you named yourself?"
But a name is not a name really. It's what you want
to be called and so someone is doing the calling.
A name could be a place where you lay down.
Where no one calls you. Where you call yourself
into a plain of lilac and sugar. I do not know
if I have every called myself. But, maybe,
there was once in the forest. All the trees were
gossiping about me. I wasn't sure what they were saying
and I wasn't sure where they learned to gossip.
But I stood there in the creek and the creek
spoke her own name and then I had space to find mine.
If I told you my name, it wouldn't be my name.

Then it would just be what you call me.

Steipereidur[1]

I have been the fish who defends fishermen.
I have been massive. I have let them
build castles on my back. I have said,
"I know it takes time to unlearn."
I have stood in front of a room and
told people my dead name just because
they asked for it. I have made my identity
into a pill to swallow. I have lied and said
I believe in cis people. I have lied and said
I believe in straight people. I have lied
and said I was human when really I was
just a great fish in a room standing
in front of fishermen. Have you ever tried
to talk to a room of fishermen?
They have harpoons. They drink their coffee
and think to themselves, "Well,
isn't that a good fish. I haven't ever
heard a fish talk so calmly." I smile
like a kitchen timer. I spit water
from my skull. They clap and are so happy
I have come to talk about being a fish.
Tomorrow they will go out and use what I said.
They will kill a fish and tell themselves
"But is this really a fish?"

---

[1]Steipereidur is the name given to a sea monster appearing on some maps in the 1600s. It was considered to be a tame kind of whale that fought other whales on behalf of fishermen.

False Flesh

I have been spreading lies.
Sometimes I walk
into a room
and I am a lie.
Sometimes a doctor
listens to my heart
and hears a whale. Sometimes
he believes my body is coming apart
and sometimes he tells me
if I run far enough
I can outrun my body.
I haven't run
in years. I have been spreading
joyous lies that I am a word or two.
That I am explainable.
That there are pronouns
that match the ways
I want to unexist.
Are there suicidal pronouns?
Pronouns that reject
capitalism? I don't know.
Someone asks again,
"Why would you want
to be referred to as 'it'?"
and I think about my love
of objects. A bowl
with a chip in it. A rusted nail
I pry from the ground.
All the souls of the objects
beaming back at me.
I have been lying
though even when I am
the "it" of your tongue.
Isn't it beautiful to lie?
Isn't it beautiful
to be lied to?

Sea / Lion

i always keep / half of myself / when i shift /
become a hybrid / of a woman / and a fire /
once someone asked / if you had / to choose a side /
/ so / i said / i'd be a woman i guess / which was / a lie /
you cannot be / something you are / not / and yet
over and over again / i am a daughter / a mouth /
/ a testicle / a bowl of ovaries / i do not have answers /
as to how a creature like me / is classified /
now / you / choose between two bodies you aren't
/ walk out into the ocean / and swim /

Let's Show Up Uninvited

Sometimes my gender has guts.
I go to the women's room
and don't think about gender.
I think about the texture
of the moon and how it's
something I'll never know.
I am so sick
of talking about bathrooms.
We were driving
and my boyfriend
points out the window
at a toilet on the side
of the road. He says,
"Look a free toilet."
I tell my lover, "What I really want
is for people to not know
what I have in my pants."
Which is not quite the truth.
I want people to feel what I feel
which is a permanent question.
"Do I belong here?"
Does he belong here? I am
a disciple of the church
of the uninvited. I once
showed up to the funeral
of someone I didn't know.
He was well-loved
and drew a great crowd.
I pretended it was a wedding
but really isn't every human ritual
a little bit of both
a funeral and a wedding?
When I was born
the doctor looked at me
and ran away.
He took a scalpel
and cut out my [   ]
then he gave me back
to my parents
and said, "It's a [   ]."
And really that's how
it's been ever since.

Helicoprion

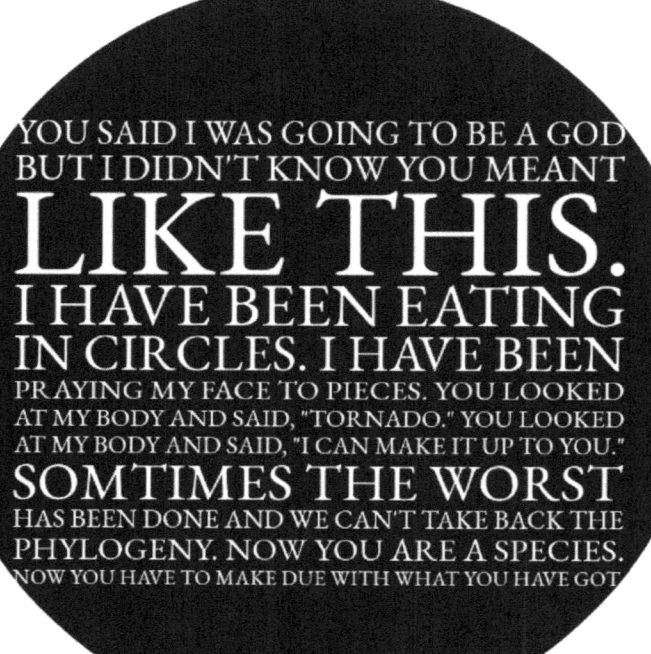

YOU SAID I WAS GOING TO BE A GOD
BUT I DIDN'T KNOW YOU MEANT
LIKE THIS.
I HAVE BEEN EATING
IN CIRCLES. I HAVE BEEN
PRAYING MY FACE TO PIECES. YOU LOOKED
AT MY BODY AND SAID, "TORNADO." YOU LOOKED
AT MY BODY AND SAID, "I CAN MAKE IT UP TO YOU."
SOMTIMES THE WORST
HAS BEEN DONE AND WE CAN'T TAKE BACK THE
PHYLOGENY. NOW YOU ARE A SPECIES.
NOW YOU HAVE TO MAKE DUE WITH WHAT YOU HAVE GOT

How to Growl / How to Grovel

Grow cold   Grow clamorous
      Remember mud   Remember rope
Give ice   Grieve guts
     Ripen fruit   Ripen meat
Get angry   Get away
     Remove pain   Remove glory
Gut the fish   Gut God
     Revive a demon   Revive a story
Grieve guts   Get angry   Get angry

RITUALS

Father

I went to a workshop on somatic poetry with CA Conrad once. They talked about having a "factory" in their head and how their rituals worked to break down the factory. Sitting in my plastic chair at the workshop I harbored my factory. I knew they could see my factory. All the little factories in our chairs.

My father has worked most of his life in a factory. He puts caps on batteries. He used to fill them with molten lead. His fingers are so callous they're almost stones. I have watched his body fall apart.

The factory is always a place of death. Lately, I feel like I'm dying. Instead of dying, I decide I have to kill my father, metaphorically of course.

Nights before I talked to my husband and said, "But I love him" after I told him some of the things my father had done. I remember a shower curtain. I remember a broom handle. Then, of course, his mantra, "I'm just going to kill myself." The time my brother spilled a bottle of beer and he smacked him hard over the head. I was maybe eight. I thought to myself, "It's not me. I'm good. It's not me." I took pride in being the one not hit.

But I do. I do love him, don't I? How and why I don't understand.

Sometimes your self turns to jelly and you are fishing for seeds.

I do not want to be so much of what I am. I am weeping in the factory.

I am doing a ritual without realizing it. I am mowing the lawn and then I am not just mowing the lawn. My father mows the lawn at my parent's house. Endlessly. Sometimes when he's too tired he'll just do it in patches. I miss my father. I miss who I thought my father was.

I listen to "Bullet with Butterfly Wings" by Smashing Pumpkins because it's a song about my father. I dig into the gravel of the words. I play it over and over.

Fresh cut grass. My head throbs. My joints all hurt. I do not want to be disabled but I also do. I want to push so hard that my body is not my body.

When I say I don't want to be disabled I don't mean it. I want to be disabled. I so badly want to let myself be disabled. I think of the week of graduate school where I walked and walked with my hip dislocated. I limped and winced. I wept in the subway and just kept pushing myself. I said, "Soon I will be a person."

The days I tried to run the street in Jim Thorpe. How hard I pushed. I invented a run-limp, a little skip. A shot doe trying to cross a street just to crumple into an asterisk.

My limbs come apart. My heart is a bag of marbles.

I mow the lawn even though I shouldn't be mowing the lawn. Even though I am exhausted. I am my father. I am my own father. He is here with me and he is not even dead but he is already a ghost. I am killing him and then I am killing his ghost.

When I am done I lay in the freshly cut grass and listen to the song some more. Try to understand which parts I believe and which parts I don't. Is the world a vampire? Do I really believe I am living inside a cage? Of course I am.

I miss you and by I miss you I mean I miss the you I thought I held in my mouth.

I always wanted him to approve of me.

Our house of rats. My father's grass stained shoes. His swollen knuckles.

I come inside and fill my mouth with a sip of Diet Coke. My father drinks diet coke all day. Case after case. The cans remind me of his teeth.

In my mouth I try to taste all the notes of the bubbling drink. I try to taste what he tastes and I hear metal and blood and bone.

I do not know if the factory is just a part of me. Sometimes I feel like it made me. I don't know how to be unmade or what I will need to do to be put back together.

I beg the factory for my father. Once we went on a tour. It was a winter day. We stood back and saw the smelter where he worked. Everything burned. I thought, "This is where my father goes every day." So much of his life in repeated motions. His bones becoming the factory and giving the factory.

I do not want to live like this. Please I do not want to live like this.

I check my work emails before bed in the dark of a room where I am dying. I try to please the closed mouths of faces on coins. I am dying. I am dying and I do not want to be dying.

I spit out the Diet Coke and feel corny. As if I could exercise a father. As if this could release everything I want to rid myself of. Then I remember that CA Conrad once soaked a piece of bread with the water of a storm and ate it. Devoured it in the face of the storm.

I am not ready to eat a storm or even my father.

I stand at the sink. Contemplate the way he always ate dinner like that. Just standing at the sink, leaning on the counter.

My whole body hurts and I take my body in my arms and I tell it I am so sorry. I am so sorry for the factory and the factory weeps and the factory starts producing as much Diet Coke as it can.

I almost do it. I almost complete the ritual. I almost call my father and tell him I remember exactly what he did to me but maybe that is another ritual.

Maybe that is only what the factory wants.

My body wants to be held. My body wants to be touched. It wants to love itself. It wants to believe I am divine. I do not know what self love looks like with a factory going. I think I am not even interested in self love. I think I am interest in destruction.

I rub my own back. I turn out all the lights and wait in the dark as if someone is coming. Swear I hear my father knocking on the door to the house.

He is not here. It is only his body with the factory still going even after he is gone.

Death

My lover tells me not to put random plants in my mouth. Fae says, "There are more poisonous ones than you might think." This is after chewing on burs I found in the yard. They grabbed onto my shirt and compression gloves. I had to through the clothes away they were so riddled with them.

I think it would be imprecise for me to say I am afraid of death. I am not, truly, that afraid of death. I am often careless with my mouth. I eat knives. I drive the car too fast.

I enjoy a lot of what death offers. I like silence when I can find it and dirt and mushrooms and demons and soil and time.

I already have a ritual about death. I steal spoon. One for every way I have died.

Once, I did a past life regression. I went into it thinking, "This is some bullshit" but I came out of it weeping. I was on my knees in my dimly lit bedroom. Hours had past listening to this recording of a man pulling me into the past. I saw myself and my lover I'm with now. We were bakers in this life. Our deaths were mundane and brilliant.

I don't know if I believe time is that slippery but maybe it is and most of us just have too many stones in us to let us slide around.

The first spoon I ever stole was from my ex. He would grab me by the hair and say, "You don't love me." This was after I had asked to please stop touching me. I was in the corner of his bedroom once and he laughed when I fell. I looked at the window and thought about throwing myself out. I thought about how great it would feel to not have to know him.

I hate how little we talk about death. I want to talk about death as much as I use a spoon.

The ritual is basically just I put the spoon in my mouth and see how long it takes for the instrument to ring. Have you ever felt a life ringing? My body is a bell.

When I used to be an altar boy my favorite role was being the bell acolyte. I rung the bell when something important was happening. Three soft rings.

After the spoon rings, I'm allowed to eat.

The most recent spoon I stole was from an Air BnB. There, we were discordant than ever. I thought I was dying. I thought I would die without you.

In the woods I left a pile of my guts. Weeks from now, after a rain, mushrooms will grow from them.

I love and hate the term "dead name" for a trans person's old name. I do feel like it's true but it also feels so sanitary. In my ritual I am dedicated to seances. "Let the dead rest" is short for "I do not want to see ghosts."

I want to see ghosts. I want to see all the ghosts.

I don't use "dead name" for myself. I say, "Another name."

I have a spoon for her. It is plastic and worn smooth.

You have to die. This is how I say it. Not "everyone dies" or "every will die" but "have to" because it is a labor in itself.

We are just driving and my lover says, "Life has meaning because we give it meaning." I don't know how we started talking about death but we talk about death often. It is something I adore about him.

I keep one of my stolen spoons with me at all times. I hope if I die people will find the spoon and be curious, then, maybe years later, reading this book, realize that the ritual is complete there.

My favorite spoon I've ever stolen is from my parent's house. I put it in my mouth each night I stayed there. Opened the window to my childhood bedroom. Let myself ring.

Mother

I've read about all kinds of rituals that have to do with birth. A tunnel to climb through. An umbilical cord balloon.

I don't need to relive this or be reborn.

This ritual is an unbirth.

I take a quail egg and wash it in the sink. Scrub with lemon soap and think hard about choosing another beginning. In an alternative biography I might start by saying, "There were ancient sharks with teeth the size of dinner knives. Centuries later a girl would cut her thumb with a dinner knife. That girl was not a girl but an entity."

Looking hard at the egg I notice its spots. The egg is blue with feathered stripes. Staring at the patterns I reflect on the quail who, for the most part, smash their eggs between the wires of their cage.

My partner and I joke, "They have no mothering instinct."

I don't think that was true for my mother. There were many times where she was tender. I remember her singing to me until I fell asleep or painting my nails after a long day's work.

In the world I grew up in, the work of a mother is a work of emptying.

There is a picture of my mother laughing outside one of my dad's rock shows. She has short hair. She looks like she could be my friend.

Placing the egg in my mouth I feel that wholeness. What it means to sew shut a genesis. No we will not begin.

Sometimes I want to ask my mom, "Would you choose to be a mother, knowing what you know now."

Her children are all nightcrawlers. We turn on lamps. We search for sugar.

You always hear celebrities saying, "I want to buy my mom a house."

The wounds my mother made hurt worse than the ones my father made even though they are so much less severe. And I wonder if it is too much to ask of a person to be a mother. Instead I find the most peace thinking of my mother as her first name and short-haired and wearing black converse similar to the ones I still wear sometimes.

Inside the egg is a sea monster. The sea monster is also me and also my mother and also my grandmother crossing an ocean of sea monsters to a land of sea monsters.

The unknown is always worth worshiping.

I put the egg in my mouth and I hold it there as long as I can. Saliva. Tongue. The urge to bite down and feel the sea monster guts in my mouth. My mother, texting me again, "How are you?" and I don't know what to say because we have grown into such separate beings.

Once, when I was fourteen, my mother yelled at me that I was selfish. I was a plastic spoon of a girl, so sick with anorexia that my body grew a soft fur not meant for sea monsters. I think of the egg I ate the next morning: scrambled with ketchup. The ketchup as blood.

I try to get myself to complete the ritual. I think I need to bite down but I can't. I keep thinking of my mother's skull and the skulls of sea monsters. Sea monsters are never children and never adults and never mothers and never daughters. They are all just sea monsters. What a relief.

The egg is wet when I remove it from my mouth. I wipe spit from my chin. The egg is whole. The egg is still whole.

Another way I might begin a story of my life is to say, "Someone became a mother and it happened over and over again." I turn and write into the question, "Why do I see gender in binaries of empty and full?"

Grandfather

When my grandfather was in the navy, he once blew up a whale. I hear the story secondhand from my father who says, "he thought the whale's voice sounded like a German submarine." I rewrite this history and decide he thought it was a sea monster. The voice bore a hole in his mind and filled his with scales and teeth and abyss. He aimed and fired as all men are taught to do.

My grandfather is from Brazil but also from Ecuador but also part Scottish. I listen to whale sounds from a YouTube video and try to conjure his journeys without ever having heard them from his own mouth. Maybe if he spoke to me, it would come out in whale sounds.

Whales use sounds just like we do. They talk and have dialects of language. They sing sometimes even just to themselves.

In the bathtub I am holding a seance for the whale my grandfather killed. I lay on my back and sing. I pretend I am a whale singing my heart out, unaware of the missile aimed at my spirit.

I want to know what my grandfather's history meant to him. What words would he have used to describe himself? If asked, "'What are you?' What word would come to mind first?" It can be a racist loaded question or, in the right mouth, a beautiful one. If asked, I would say, "I am a sea monster" or, maybe, "I am a whale."

I imagine my grandfather saying, "I am a man" but deep down wanting to say, "I am a sea monster."

I wait in the tub until my skin is pruned and my heart is a plum. I get out slowly so I don't faint. Sit in the tub and then pretend I am the missile. Helpless in the ways I'm going to tear apart a voice. I slip out of the tub and detonate. I eat my plum heart. Juice drips down my arms.

My grandfather lives in the silence of the bathroom. I hear the squeak of his cane against the floor. He does not have anything he can manage to tell me. The whale is there too. The whale cries. The whale forgives him and then so do I.

Wedding

I thought we were having a wedding. Instead, I was holding an urgency. Come here and love me. Tell me you will love me until I am dust.

What unites queerness and straightness is that they're both about death. Deaths of too much and not enough.

I never stopped to think, "How would I marry myself?"

I tell you, "I'm so sorry" but what I mean is, "I don't even know if I wanted to get married. I was just scared of losing you."

Marriage is a system built on the bartering of genders for stolen land and stolen blood. Haven't you ever looked at a mansion though and thought, "That is so beautiful"? Imagined yourself and your objects enshrined among the walls?

My wedding involves a thrift store wedding dress. I will live inside it until I feel my bride gender. I want to nestle there. I want to feel taken.

I lay down in the yard and then get into a bridge pose. I want bugs to use my back and body for travel. They do. All kinds of pill bugs and grass-hoppers and then the glorious spider. I want to hold it long enough for the spider to build webs but my arms are weak and give our.

A good ritual should touch the limits of the body. Straining arms or attention or your gender. The dress feels like it's getting tighter. I want to cut it off of me. I start to cry.

In the yard, I go to talk to the rusted ladder. I put it up against the side of the house and I climb on the roof. My lover is asleep but I pretend he is a cloud. I reach and reach and can't pull him down. Then, I wait until I see my own features in the clouds. I fish a chim down. Put my face back togeth-er.

I'm wondering if a wedding is not something that can happen all at once or if it maybe is an action trying to force something unnamable to happen all at once. I feel the gift of my gender after hours of the dress holding me still. I worship the dress. I worship my gender.

When it's time to remove the dress I think of destruction. I use the craft scissors, the ones that are slightly rusted. I pretend I am my lover, cutting me out of the dress. His careful hands. Can I love myself like he would love me?

Once naked, I look at the husk of my gender. I fold my gender up and burry the dress. I am still naked. This is the most important part.

I spend the rest of the day naked. Bathe and dream of what my genders are doing now that they're married. Do they find new routines? Is everything changed? Is everything gone?

Wild Mirror

I once ate a mirror like an apple.
Glass in my teeth.
Spit blood in the yard.
Each drop of blood
became a raspberry bush.
I picked them in the early summer.
Ate myself to death.
Buried myself. Became
a well of blood. A new family
moved into my body.
They braided garlic
and hung it on the windows.
The new family left
and another came and another.
In my well
the mirror reformed itself.
Stared down at me
and begged me,
"Look." I would not look.
I would not let myself
be captured not even
for a glance. "This is
mine," I said about my blood
even though it was pumped
through the house
and poured from every faucet.

Self-Portrait as What Was Taken

Eyes. Teeth. Scales.
Forked Tail. Like the other fish.
A dress. Golden age. Golden light.
Softness. Stillness.
A land before vessels. Before
the ocean was named. A body before
fear started to classify it.
Curiosity. All inhabitants of the town.
Sinking ships. Transmogrifying.
The swing set. My testes. My dick.
Your dick. The door off its hinges.
The nighttime. The front porch.
The soybeans we plucked. My thongs.
My mouth. My appetite. My fat.
More of my fat. All of my fat.
Skin. Tea leaves. A mini fridge.
Virginity. The concept of virginity.
The violence of virginity.
Agency. Wanderlust. My hair.
My fingers. My tongue. My Oldsmobile.
My name. My gender.
My blood. The last thin mint.

Mother Whale

You're telling me you've never made a man scream?
Well, my love, that is not living. I go out
with my skull cut open, ocean gushing
onto the deck of a ship. The men run.

The men let let sounds like ripped cows.
They cry for their mothers and I tell them,
"I am your mother now." They cover their faces.
They plead, begging, "Let my real mother
come and turn me into a loaf of bread."

Once, I went to a conference of mother whales.
The other whales shared stories of all the men's
fears. I collected them like necklaces. Like pearls.
I let them turn caramel in my heart.

Don't be afraid of your evil. Cultivate it.
Cling to it. Wrap your tongue around it.
What are you afraid will emerge
if you let yourself hate them?

How Free Do You Want to Be?

I want to be evergreen in my teeth.
I do not believe in
small changes
over time. I believe in
catastrophic science. I believe
melt-in-the-mouth logic.
Let's not tell people we are human
anymore. Let's tell people
we are from another dimension
not sent or called for
but simply arrived.
Have you considered
what it would look like
to remove meaning?
To re-classify your blood?
I have stopped putting "blue"
in my bios. Instead I say,
"I am a poet and this is my butter."
Bruising from fucking all night.
We watch a horror movie
and leave the doors unlocked afterward.
I tell you "I am not scared of other humans."
This is a choice I make
each and every day
even after I have watched
a men carve me
like a leg of lamb.
The basement was cool
to the touch. Sometimes memories
come up for air
and I don't know if I should
cut them into quarters
and devour them
or if I should tell them
they happened to another body.
A body that lived in a test tube.
That is not where my body lives.
What if freedom
is a word that always calls
the border? Always says,

"Here is what I escaped."
I do not want to be escaped.
I want to be echoing. I want to be
the taste of sassafras. I believe
in burying freedom with flowers
and telling her
"We have turned the box
to air."

Brethmechin

Once on the beach I cracked open a clam by throwing it against the rocks. I wanted to find a pearl. I was ten and chubby. Instead, inside, I saw a baby. The baby was small. It fit in the palm of my hand. I was immediately aware that the baby was myself. I felt sick and scared. I wanted to put the baby back. I didn't know how or why the baby had gotten there. I wept and so did the baby. The shell was broken. There was no way to go back. I buried the shell and the baby in the sand. I wiped my hands. I worried I would die, that somehow I had killed myself and a wave would happen through time. I did not die but the baby grew in the weeks we left the beach. The baby became a sea monster who still swims to this day. He has flippers and fur. He doesn't know anything about me. I wonder what he would have become if he were left to develop. Would he have been a pearl in a necklace I was meant to wear? I am still a keeper of this secret and now you are too. Do not tell anyone unless you must. Then just tell your lover. We all know that lovers become each other's limbs. If I met the monster, I would feed him. I would bring handfuls of gems. I would say, "I am so sorry." He might weep again or he might scream. He might devour me. Drag me into the ocean. Place me inside the mouth of a giant clam.

Self-Portrait as What Everyone Else Sees

I love the word "faggot."
I love to be
a faggot.
Sometimes it feels
like telling the truth.
I don't want
to be easy to understand.
I don't want to explain
why or how.
I want to be
as dangerous as
the government thinks I am.
A deviant. A lost girl.
A receptacle. A good one.
A problem. A burden.
Whatever you want.
Whatever you don't want.
A demon. A witch.
A statistic. A cripple. I guess
sometimes people believe
I'm a woman and I think
that's interesting. Sometimes people think
I'm a man and somehow
that kind of hurts my feelings
like dear God don't let
me be a man.
I don't know if
people see the difference
between boy and man.
I know sometimes people say,
"Sir uh I mean miss,"
and then they stare, trying to
puzzle me out.
I am not just the dis-identification
of myself
but the confusion that comes back
to the onlooker like
"what do I know is true?"

Kraken

Do you believe me when I tell you I have seen the sun's twin?
Deep in the black ocean there is a point where the darkness
is so rich it becomes heaven. I go there to worship

my wrongness. My underworlds. I hold them.
Cut myself open there to see all the tangled necklaces
and rusted needle buttons. The sun has a face like

a grandmother I never met. It is raining and a thunder storm
is on the way. I am telling you it is alright and the rain comes
like great globs of blood. I do not tell anyone I am a kraken.

Instead, I fit myself into language other people need
to hold onto me. I call my mother even though I don't want to.
I cannot tell her what I want to tell her which is

that I found the other sun because of my father.
I go there every time I see them all together. A living room
full of eyes. I think of standing at the bathroom sink

and washing my face over and over. I do not want
to be salvaged or saved. I want to be sunk. I want to drown
and for no one to find the body. Let them say,

"We do not know what it was." Let them make their
glorious mythology. Blame me. Blame themselves.
But then I think of my sun. We think too much of trauma

as the pain defining us. No. I will not be dictionary
or risk factor anything. I will look at the organs I've grown.
The shadows who said, "Look we are alive."

How Long Have You Known You Were A [   ]?

There are two answers that feel possible.
I always was or I never was.

>   Either a monster is inherent
>   or invented
by fear
or craving.

Aren't we all   invented by the fears or desires of others?

I don't want to be.   I don't want to have been.

>   Have you ever refused?

>   I don't mean a spoonful
>   I mean a hunger strike.

I mean starving. Skeleton. Stone museum.

Let's not get carried away now.
>   You love your face, don't you?

Now
take the face out of your face?
>   Do you still love it?

Mermaid in a Glass of Water or Alternative Self-History

When I was born the doctor looked down
and saw a fishtail where my legs should be.
My mom and dad took me home
in a glass of water.
Neither of them knew what to do with
a mermaid.
You probably think of mermaids
as beautiful
but we are terrifying. My teeth grew
like broken bottles. Jagged and twisted.
They fed me stones. First just spoonfuls
of sand and then pebbles and then
palm-sized rocks.
I feasted. They let me go into the river
when I was only five. They didn't know
what else to do with me. Neither cried.
My legs always lived somewhere else.
In a dinosaur fossil or lost
in the sea between blood and water.
I saw to the sea. I live here still. I kiss
every gender of merperson. My femme
is fluid and fearless. I have never once cut my hair.

Emergency-ing

A monster is a calamity document.
I signed my name on your face
and we made things official.

When I promised to be a being
I didn't know I was saying,
"Now everyone will see me."

Where seeing means inspecting
and where inspecting means dissecting.
"I know exactly what you mean,"

from the mouth of someone
who does not know anything
about what I mean. Once I called

911. It was the dead of night.
I had fallen in the hallway. I lived alone.
I curled up like a tongue. Could not speak

thought to myself, "How does anyone
speak?" Checkers on the ceiling.
A toad turning to a whistle in my mouth.

Great Serpent

Let's feed our names back to our mothers.
I don't mean my human mother I mean
my monster mother of the abyss.
I will walk around with a plate of eyes
trying to coax the snake from the water.
She is known to live in the crooked elbow
of the deep. Sleeping there, she dreams
abundance. Of cities in which no streets
have names and no people have names.
I want to go there to be disappeared.
To be re-hatched from a wandering clam.
The pearl is the knot where weddings live.
A pyre for the celebration. The snake singing
a hymn about the rebirth after rebirth.
The unbirth where I go to call myself
one direction at a time. Winds like sisters
weave a coffin for my hair and then one
for each hand. There are not enough
places to hide a word. Sometimes the name
returns and says, "Here is how you were legible."
I return to say, "You only thought you saw me."

Sea Monster Family Tree

Haven't you ever watched your father eat his father?
I have seen my mother peeled as an onion
and her mother in a catacomb of fish.
My trees fall in circuses. I spend all night
trying to find a cousin or a great grandfather
who was a sea monster.
I find several but their pictures
were drawn by sailors and sailor never know
how to capture the glow of our eyes.
I make sacrifices to textbook gods.
Imagine a sea shell fill of elders
who might speak and say, "Little sea monster
we are not afraid of your terror."
I do not find them. Their voices have riptides.
They tear me apart. Do they ask me
or do I ask myself to walk on land?
A better life is a myth we are all dying of
and yet there's still the truth to it.
The sweetness of fresh bread. The bread
is a sister or a mother or a father without hands.
I go down to the water and try
to spill out all of my blood but it keeps
coming back. Pulse of the tide.

44

Sea Devil

It isn't fun being a traitor anymore.
I want to be celebrated. I want to
have a parade on my tongue.
Instead I arrive at a precipice
overlooking a family vacation.
Someone is saying, "Let's turn the president
into a frog." I think "Thank God."
You know there is a monk seal
and then there is a devil.
The devil comes from the depths
of our imaginations. The devil has
a chapel in his breakfast bowl.
I favor the tall tale. My partner is joking
when he says I'm spineless but
there's a truth that I'm terrified of.
The truth that sometimes I let people
make their mythologies of me. I say yes
I am the demon-talker. I am the legless
creature who doesn't know how to sing with you.
I want most to be invited
to parties I won't even go to.
Decline the moon and the sun
will come with all her hair on fire.

Carta Marina

/
If we were going to turn back

you would have needed to be immortal.

I start counting years.   Reading palms.

You are not allowed
to die before me.

The joint deaths
of massive stars.   I said we search
for gold
but you heard "God"

and you were right.

A crustacean heart.   The affliction of every man
who has tried to sing
into the mouth of a gender.

I buy an air conditioner.   Feed it milk.

Your feet never once

touched the dirt.
Walk on water.
Walk on walk.   Walk on skeletons.

Antennae aching to have
their white muscles sucked clean.

/
I put a compass in your chest
and you still couldn't find the star.

We road a ship to a land with the wrong name.
The wrong name was all we had so

we had to go around speaking
a language that didn't exist until it did.

Isn't the story of sea cats? How they
dance in the shadow of the one word

they keep to themselves? Do the words
we don't say die with us or are they

absorbed somehow into the water.
Taken on every wave? I want to believe

they are not gone. Tell me, what if we
decide to try to go back home

and everyone calls home a sound
our tongues can't make?

/
Meeting another one of your kind
            where "kind" refers to "wanderer"
and not bodies.

                        The sea birthed
                   my oldest skin
            but I am not sure about this one.

            This form feels
like a sheath.
Is there liberation
in being unknown?   A grotto
                                where teeth fall
            as rain.

We do not need to speak a word

            just stare into each other's
wild sundial eyes
and ask, "How many have you eaten today?"

You say, "Eight" and
            I say, "Nothing."

"Let us go then and find
                    some men together."

/
Please tell me I have a cathedral at the bottom of the ocean
where fish go to worship in my flesh.

Organ and organ song.   I used to float downriver
                        in the summer
                when everyone is so coriander.

        I want to be feasted on.
I want my identity to feed you.

            Paper plate love.   Paper moon ghost.

Paper plane vacation.

        We kept a body beneath the staircase
just on the off chance someone might want
to stop believing in God.

                I had a whole ocean
            I never told you about and you thought you could
put my name on your tongue
and devour me.

/
There is nothing more dangerous
than naming
a border.

Here is where
the self begins.

Here is where starts
the sea of monsters.

Here is how to love
and how to destroy.

Here is my skin
and here is yours.

I am good and beautiful
and you are a monster.

You are good and beautiful
I am a monster.

There are mermaids
calling the ship

towards the rocks.
There are rocks turning

into creatures.
Everything has eyes
out here.
/
Can you find me in this soup can?

Can you find me in this ocean?

In the aerial view I am the bird's eye.

Bone in the broth.

If you tried to diagram me

I would undiagram the diagram.

An arrow pointing to my queerness

and then pointing towards a gap in my teeth.

There is a Jupiter place we can go

to not have any skin.

I swear I used to be able

to hear the waves from my house.

About the Author

Robin Gow (it/fae/he & él y elle) is a trans poet, witch, and community educator. It grew up in Kutztown, Pennsylvania and lives with his partner Rain and their menagerie of animals on unceded Lenape land also called Allentown Pennsylvania. Awarded the Jerry Cain and Scott James Creative Writing Fellow, Gow earned faer MFA in Creative Writing from Adelphi University where fae also taught as a professor of English.

Robin is the author of several chapbooks, most recently Monstrous Cartography, as well as the poetry collections *Our Lady of Perpetual Degeneracy*, *the moon crawls on all fours*, and *Lanternfly August*.

In addition to writing poetry, Gow also writes Young Adult and Middle-Grade books. It is the author of YA novels in verse, A Million Quiet Revolutions, and Ode to My First Car with FSG Books for Young Readers, and Dear Mothman with Abrams Books. Fae has earned starred reviews from Publisher's Weekly, Kirkus, School Library Journal, and more.

Gow works as a community educator around LGBTQIA2+ and disability justice.